This book belongs to:

- -

- -

Importance of good deeds in Islam

In Islam, doing good deeds is an important part of a Muslim's faith and practice. There are many benefits of doing good deeds:

1. Allah is happy with us:
   - The main reason for doing good deeds in Islam is for Allah's happiness. Acts of kindness and righteousness are a way of coming closer to Allah.
2. Rewards in the hereafter:
   - Every act of kindness or charity will be rewarded in the afterlife.
3. Good for our soul:
   - Acts of kindness and charity cleanse the heart and strengthen our connection with Allah.
4. Following the example of Prophet Muhammad (peace be upon him):
   - Our Prophet's (PBUH) life is an example of compassion, generosity, and kindness, encouraging believers to follow in his footsteps.

5. Forgiveness:
- Islam teaches that good deeds can help erase past sins.

6.Setting an example for others:
- Doing good deeds inspires others to do the same too.

In Islam, doing good deeds is important for our own faith and also helps those around us.

In this book, you will find a few examples of good deeds, along with their rewards.

بِسْمِ اللهِ الرَّحْمٰنِ الرَّحِيْمِ

I can...
Recite the Quran

The Prophet (PBUH) said, "Whoever recites a letter from the Book of Allah, he will get a good deed, and a good deed gets a ten-fold reward. I do not say that Alif-Lam-Mim is one letter, but Alif is a letter, Lam is a letter, and Mim is a letter." (At-Tirmidhi)

I can...
Pray my 5 daily salah

The Prophet (PBUH) said, "The five daily prayers from Jumu'ah to Jumu'ah are a forgiveness of the sins committed between those times as long as you don't do major sins." (Bukhari)

I can...
Smile

The Prophet (PBUH) said, "Smiling in your brother's face is an act of charity" (At-Tirmidhi)

I can...
Fast

The Prophet (PBUH) said: "Every deed of the son of Adam will be multiplied between ten and seven hundred times. Allah (SWT) said: "Except fasting. It is for Me and I shall reward it because My servant gives up his desires and his food for My sake." (Sahih Muslim)

I can...
Do dhikr

Dhikr (or remembrance of Allah) is an easy way to gain lots of good deeds. Allah says in the Quran: "Therefore remember Me (by praying, glorifying, etc.) and I will remember you"
(Surah Al-Baqarah (2:152))
Example of dhikr: SubhanAllah, Alhamdulillah, La Ilaha IllAllah, Allahu Akbar

I can...
Visit the sick

The Prophet (PBUH) said: "When a Muslim visits a sick Muslim at dawn, seventy thousand angels keep on praying for him till dusk. If he visits him in the evening, seventy thousand angels keep on praying for him till the morning; and he will have (his share of) reaped fruits in Jannah."
(At-Tirmidhi)

I can...
Be kind to my parents

Allah is pleased with the ones who are kind to their parents. The Prophet (PBUH) said: "The pleasure of the Lord is in the pleasure of the father/mother, and the displeasure of the Lord is in the displeasure of the father/mother."
(At-Tirmidhi)

I can... Share

A good muslim must share with his/her friends and family, and wish goodness for them. Our Prophet (PBUH) said: "In order to be a Muslim, wish for your fellow Muslims that which you wish for yourself."
(At-Tirmidhi)

I can...
Be kind to animals

The Prophet (PBUH) said, "There is a reward for helping any living creature." (Bukhari)

I can...
Plant a tree

The Prophet (PBUH) said, "Whenever Muslims plant a tree, they will earn the reward of charity because of the food that comes from it"
(Sahih Muslim)

I can...
Give charity

The Quran says that those who give charity will have the reward of paradise and forgiveness for sins. You can donate money, food, water and volunteer with charities too.

I can...
Say salaam

The Prophet (PBUH) said that giving the greeting of salaam to those whom you know and those whom you do not know is one of the best deeds in Islam (Bukhari)

I can...
Talk to my family

The Prophet (PBUH) said: "He who believes in Allah and the Last Day, let him maintain good relations with family members (Bukhari). If you do this, Allah will reward you with a long and blessed life.

I can...
Help my neighbour

The Prophet (PBUH) said: "Treating your neighbors with kindness and being a good neighbor will result in an increase in your share of daily bread and the development of towns."
(Mustadrak al-Wasa'il)

I can...
Go to the masjid

The Prophet (PBUH) said: "Whoever goes to the masjid in the morning and evening, Allah will make for him a place in Paradise for every morning and evening." (Bukhari and Muslim)

I can...
Do dawah

The Prophet (PBUH) said: "Whoever guides someone to goodness will have a reward like one who did it."
(Sahih Muslim)

I can...
Donate my old toys

Donating your things is a form of charity, and charity is rewarded by Allah.

I can...
Clean the environment

As muslims, it is our duty to save water, not cut down trees unnecessarily and not to pollute the environment.

I can...
Do hajj

Hajj is one of the five pillars of Islam. The reward for Hajj is the promise of Paradise, and the forgiveness of all your sins.

I can...
Clean the masjid

The masjid is a house of Allah, so whoever cleans it and makes it easy for people to pray there will be rewarded.

I can...
Be kind to my grandparents

In Islam, grandparents are just like our own parents, so we have to be kind to them and take care of them too.

I can...
Stop backbiting

Backbiting is when you talk about someone when they are not around (behind their back). It is not allowed in Islam and if anyone stays away from doing this, they will be rewarded by Allah.

I can...
Do umrah

Performing umrah will help forgive your sins and increase you in wealth and blessings.

I can...
Clear a path

Removing a stone or any harmful object from a path is a type of charity.

I can...
Memorize the Quran

Memorizing the Quran makes you rise to higher levels of Jannah, and even your parents are rewarded. If you read and memorize the Quran, it will give you company on the Day of Judgement and in the grave.

I can...
Learn about Prophet Muhammad (PBUH)

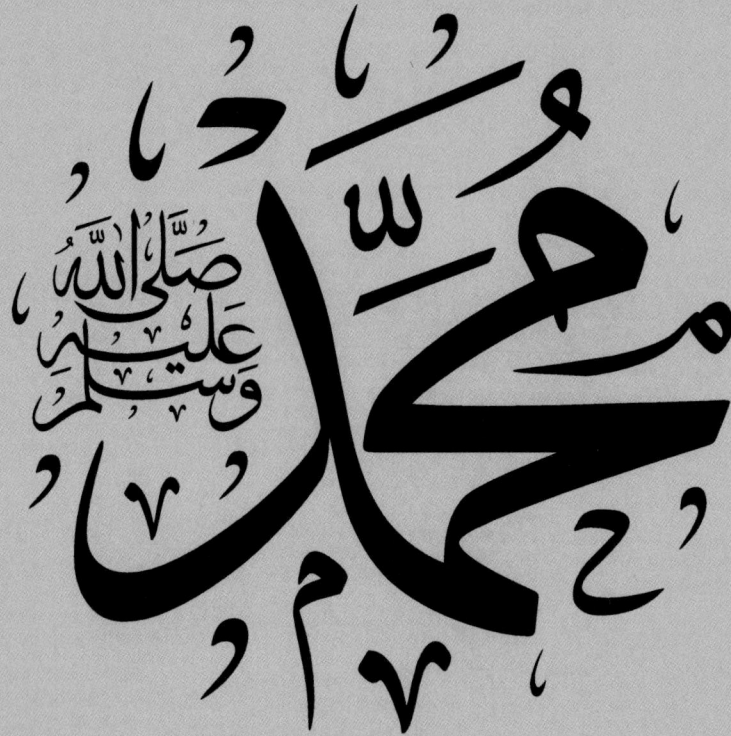

محمد صلى الله عليه وسلم

Our Prophet Muhammad (PBUH) is the best role model for muslims.
Learning about his life and habits will make us feel closer to him.

I can...
Memorize the Names of Allah

The Prophet (PBUH) said: "Allah has ninety-nine names, and whoever knows them will go to Paradise." (Bukhari)

I can...
Learn about Islam

The Prophet (PBUH) said: "Whoever follows a path to seek knowledge, Allah will make the path to Jannah easy for them."
(Sahih Muslim)

I can...
Control my anger

Whoever controls their anger when they feel really angry is rewarded with happiness on the Day of Judgement.

I can...
Send blessings on
The Prophet (PBUH)

The Prophet (PBUH) said: "Whoever sends salah upon me once, Allah (SWT) will send salah upon him tenfold, and will erase ten sins from him, and will raise him ten degrees in status."
(Sunan an-Nasa'i)

I can...
Do voluntary acts of worship

If you want extra good deeds, you can fast and pray more than what is required. For example, fasting on Mondays and Thursdays and praying Tahajjud (The voluntary night prayer before Fajr).

Made in the USA
Monee, IL
25 March 2025

14521829R00021